THIS BOOK BELONGS TO:

_____

_____

Dear Moms, Dads, and Lovely Kiddos!

Welcome to the thrilling world of Monster Trucks! In this coloring book, you will delight in a variety of high-quality illustrations showcasing these powerful vehicles. Get ready to embark on an adventure filled with excitement and creativity as you bring these monster trucks to life with your colors. Let your imagination run wild as you explore the roaring engines and bold designs of these incredible machines. Get set to rev up your coloring skills and enjoy the ride!

Your feedback means the world to us! If you and your little ones enjoyed the Monster Trucks coloring book, would you mind taking a moment to leave us a review? Your thoughts help us continue to create fun and engaging experiences for young fans of monster trucks. Thank you for your support!

Made in United States
Orlando, FL
14 October 2024

52630462R00057